T0117835

Still Another Day

Aún

PABLO NERUDA
Still Another Day

TRANSLATED BY WILLIAM O'DALY

COPPER CANYON PRESS

Copyright 1971 by Pablo Neruda and Heirs of Pablo Neruda

Translation copyright 1984, 2005 by William O'Daly

All rights reserved

Cover photo by Geostock.
Designed by Phil Kovacevich.
Printed in the United States of America

Copper Canyon Press is in residence at Fort Worden State Park in Port
Townsend, Washington, under the auspices of Centrum Foundation.
Centrum is a gathering place for artists and creative thinkers from around
the world, students of all ages and backgrounds, and audiences seeking
extraordinary cultural enrichment.

LIBRARY OF CONGRESS CATALOGING-IN-PUBLICATION DATA

Neruda, Pablo, 1904–1973.
  [Aún. English & Spanish]
  Still another day = Aún / by Pablo Neruda ; translated by William O'Daly.
      p. cm.
  ISBN 1-55659-224-8 (pbk. : alk. paper)
  I. Neruda, Pablo, 1904–1973. Aún. I. Title: Aún. II. O'Daly, William.
III. Title.
  PQ8097.N4A913 2005
  861'.62—DC22

                        2005003263

SECOND EDITION

COPPER CANYON PRESS
Post Office Box 271
Port Townsend, Washington 98368
www.coppercanyonpress.org

Translator's Acknowledgments

If the spirit of this translation captures the spirit of the original, the community of hands that helped to build it a home in English must share in the credit. Dr. Sergio Bocaz-Moraga, Professor of Spanish Emeritus at Eastern Washington University, was especially generous in relating the connotations of certain words that a non-Chilean speaker of Spanish might miss. Dr. Perry Higman, Professor of Spanish and Director of the EWU Honors Program, and Dr. José A. Elgorriaga, Professor Emeritus of Spanish at California State University, Fresno, offered indispensable suggestions and thoughtful encouragements. Philip Levine commented on an early draft and offered helpful suggestions and inspiration, the latter in the classroom and through his fine translations of Jaime Sabines. I also extend my thanks to family and friends who supported my efforts with their faith and inexhaustible patience.

Twenty years ago, *Still Another Day* was the first to be published in my series of six books by Neruda. The response from Neruda's readers across the English-speaking world and beyond has been generous and warm, endowed with a camaraderie so many of us feel with this Chilean Nobel laureate who fulfilled his commitment to readers and to all people, even his lifelong critics and enemies, in an uncompromising yet profoundly humane way.

To Copper Canyon Press and its remarkable staff, I extend my gratitude that defies adequate expression, for their commitment to this project over the many years and for their gracious spirit and expertise.

The participation of all increased the pleasure of the task, and infused it with greater precision and veracity. Any errors or inadequacies in the translations are my own.

INTRODUCTION

Aún (*Still Another Day*) is Pablo Neruda's farewell to the Chilean people, to all people who have discovered the affirmative power of his poetry. More aware than ever of his mortality when he wrote these 433 verses, over two days in July 1969, Neruda celebrates the gift of having one more day in which to sing his farewell song. (*Aún* literally means "and yet.") Readers familiar with his earlier poetry, especially the magnificent epic *Canto General,* will recognize themes that became "unrelenting human occupations" throughout his life: the human spirit, his personal commitments, the birth of his country, the earth.

Even so, in *Aún* the earth is no longer primarily the feminine principle that rejuvenates life: it is the ultimate giver and taker-away of life. In coming to terms with his personal relationship to the earth, Neruda invokes the Araucanian Indians, the conquistadores who tried to enslave them, the people and places of his childhood, the epic poet Alonso de Ercilla, the Atacama Desert, La Frontera, Isla Negra, the smells and sounds and sights of the poor marketplace. Solitude and silence ultimately conjoin to become a source of creation. The empty net that was the young poet's self, capturing essential qualities of experience in the first canto of "Alturas de Macchu Picchu" ("The Heights of Macchu Picchu," from *Canto General*), has vanished: "No, the net of the years doesn't unweave: there is no net." The black cup held by exhausted urban man in the third canto of "Macchu Picchu" finds another form here in "the raised wine" that flutters like a butterfly in his grandfather's hand. The reader might experience this long poem as a sequence of distillates or perhaps crystallizations, clarified visions of recurrent themes, charged with the poet's urgent need to consider them one last time.

~

On September 23, 1973, Pablo Neruda died of the cancer that we cannot be certain he knew he had. If he did not know, it was because he chose not to acknowledge it to himself. (It's been reported that he skipped a second appointment with a specialist in Santiago, which might have alerted him early on to the presence of prostate cancer.) But also, those closest to the situation, particularly his wife, Matilde, seem to have felt that his chances of survival would be better if he were to receive cancer treatments under the pretense of combatting a less lethal disorder. Whatever the case, we know that he spoke and wrote to friends about his steadily declining health over the four years prior to his death, and he lived just long enough to hear that the culmination of his thirty-year struggle to gain political representation for Chilean workers had collapsed in a puddle of blood. The bullet-riddled body of his friend Salvador Allende, who had been popularly elected to the presidency in 1970, lay in the Palacio de la Moneda, and the military was in control. This experience must have recalled the death of another friend, Federico García Lorca, executed by a Falangist firing squad one month after the outbreak of the Spanish Civil War. But while Lorca's death helped to inspire the poems in *España en el corazón* (*Spain in My Heart,* 1937), and while the Spanish Republican cause had awakened a sense of patria (motherland)* in a young Neruda, the military coup very likely hastened don Pablo's death.

In Santiago his funeral procession attracted the notice of hundreds of people who asked who was passing. Hearing that it was Pablo Neruda, many ignored the rain and the soldiers' automatic rifles to join the procession as it made its way to the General

Cemetery, opposite the square along Avenida de la Paz. By the time the mourners and admirers arrived at the cemetery, they were singing. Someone called out Neruda's name, bidding their comrade farewell. Someone else answered aloud for him, saying he was present, now and always.

~

Neruda was raised in the southern town of Temuco, in a region ceded to the Chilean government by the Araucanian Indians in 1881. As a boy he spent hours rambling in the surrounding rain-soaked forests and on occasion accompanied his stern father, the driver of a ballast train, on long trips into the wild Andes. For three centuries this region south of the Bío-Bío River, known as La Frontera, had been the stronghold of the Araucanos (specifically, the Mapuche) who struggled with the Spanish for their independence and their land. Ever since don Pedro de Valdivia, an officer under Pizarro in Peru, marched a caravan of soldiers and indian slaves south to establish Santiago, in 1541, and confronted the Araucanos at the Bío-Bío, the Araucanos had sustained the reputation of being indomitable warriors. Alonso de Ercilla played a significant role in spreading that reputation with his epic poem, *La Araucana* (1569). Neruda looked to Ercilla as the "founder" of Chile, and loosely identified himself as a fellow *poeta del pueblo* (poet of the people) engaged in re-creating his country's birth.

Patria is typically translated as "fatherland," and occasionally as "homeland." I translate it here as "motherland" because *fatherland* has acquired fascist connotations, especially since World War II. *Motherland* emphasizes the sense of one's country as nurturer and protector, as well as a homeland to which one willingly offers allegiance. It also suggests a bond between the human nation and Mother Earth in the feminine principle. *La patria* expresses the feminine.

The Spanish Civil War compelled Neruda to align himself with a popular political movement; he returned to Chile filled with a longing to rediscover the people and their roots. Their roots were his roots. In the rich loam of Araucanian lore he came to know a race that refused to be conquered by the conquistadores and the Incas, and that only succumbed to the *chilenos* after nearly a century of resistance. One of the unnamed heroes in *Aún,* the young chief Lautaro, once a groom to Valdivia, killed his master in a battle that helped to delay conquest until 1884. Ever defiant and self-determined, the Mapuche ("people of the earth") allowed their animal tales and myths to absorb the influence of Spanish mythology while their customs and beliefs remained essentially unchanged. In *Canto General* the poet re-creates the history of these people as they become for him the *árbol de pueblo* (tree of the people), the collective voice that can never be destroyed because new leaves, each one representing a human being, regenerate the immortal trunk. The old leaves carry their story back into the ground, and the poet hears their story in the present. Neruda identifies with the trunk, the leaves, and the earth. But while in *Canto General* he distinguishes between his actions and the ravages of modern man, in *Aún* he shares in the guilt: "the blood no longer reigned in Arauco: / the kingdom of theft had arrived / and we were the thieves."

Neruda claimed that he was personally grateful to the Araucanian resistance for creating La Frontera and enabling his father and his stepmother (his birth mother died when he was two months old) to live on the edge of civilization. Though the indians only occasionally came into town to sell their goods and his contact with them was minimal, he was captivated by the sounds of Mapuche words, redolent of wild plants. The smell of wood, the sounds of an ax sinking into an oak, the shiny bark of araucarias, the hammers ringing out from the blacksmiths' shops all became powerful memories for him as the years went by. The poet captures these sensations in this book of "little symphonies," as they are called by Dr. Sergio Bocaz-Moraga, who has lived and spent a good deal of time in Temuco. Of *Aún* he says, "... The poet summons the magical, musical sounds contained in the humble Mapuche language ...the rumors, the smells, the beloved landscapes and seascapes." This musical analogy is meant to explain neither the form of the individual sections nor the overall structure of this long poem, but to cast it as a masterful enactment of the poet's desire — after his earlier, more effusive poetry — to achieve a "guided spontaneity" in his work, which the reader can hear in the beautifully orchestrated themes and tones that shape one another as wind and rain, sun and moon shape the land and the sea.

This small book contains to varying degrees nearly all of Neruda's obsessive themes juxtaposed to strike surprising harmonies and contrasts that are intimately related by the sad intensity of the language. The reader hears invocations of the earth, lyrical celebrations of people and places, simple statements of belief, intense whispers and bitter cries sometimes reminiscent of the brooding character of the dark Frontera. If the phonetic imitations of the Mapuche language escape most readers, we still can hear deep resonances in the place-names so integral to the Araucanos and Neruda himself. His personal symbology often rhymes with elements of Mapuche symbology, as in the invocations of the Aysén waterfall and the Osorno volcano, a source of magical southern fire (*cherufe* in Mapuche). The poet blends the sounds to create in Spanish the aural effects of his imagery:

> Los días no se descartan ni se suman, son abejas
> que ardieron de dulzura o enfurecieron
> el aguijón: el certamen continúa,
> van y vienen los viajes desde la miel al dolor.
>
> (XVIII)

The contrasting hard "i" and middle "a" and hollow "o" sounds running through the contrapuntal rhythm of the lines carry the emotional impact of distance that accompanies the realization of days not "discarded or collected" in a life journeying between "honey and pain."

> Fue temblorosa la noche de setiembre.
> Yo traía en mi ropa
> la tristeza del tren que me traía
> cruzando una por una las provincias.

(XVII)

Hear how the repetition of *traía* and *una* and the series of monosyllables counterpointed with three- and four-syllable words imitate the sounds of a steam-driven train crossing the provinces, how the lines evoke a sense of distance now tempered by expectation. *Aún* is composed of a masterful integration of sound and experience, and yet, as in the sprawling *Canto,* it is the poet's self that harmonizes the diverse themes and musicalities.

I first came across this book in the Spanish-language section of the Stanislaus County Library in Modesto, California, in 1975. I had not seen a single book of poems by Neruda written after 1962. *Aún* appeared to be an isolated enactment of his belief that "poetry is an action... in which there join as equal partners solitude and solidarity, emotion and action, the nearness to oneself, the nearness to mankind and to all the secret manifestations of nature" (Nobel lecture). The poet had drawn one final breath with which to say goodbye, to deliver a last will and testament that expressed the hope that his poetry and his life had served the "never-completed struggle" to allow people their own destinies. I was unaware then that he was writing *Fin de mundo* (*World's End*), which he described to one critic as a "bitter" book, "a kind of nightmare about the cruelty and evil of the twentieth century," during the time he composed this small gem of wisdom and love.

I was also unaware that Neruda had sustained his last breath through fourteen books of poems, eight of which sat on his desk nearly ready for publication at the time of the military coup. He had planned to publish all eight on his seventieth birthday. Indeed, *Aún* is not an isolated work, but one that launches the poet on a personal expedition through a vast range of themes and styles in search of his deepest roots. Along the way, he reaffirms the need for common respect among people and takes solace in the regenerative powers of the land, the wave, and the day.

WILLIAM O'DALY
AUTUMN 2004

Still Another Day

Aún

I

Hoy es el día más, el que traía
una desesperada claridad que murió.
Que no lo sepan los agazapados:
todo debe quedar entre nosotros,
día, entre tu campana
y mi secreto.

Hoy es el ancho invierno de la comarca olvidada
que con una cruz en el mapa y un volcán en la nieve
viene a verme, a volverme, a devolverme el agua
desplomada en el techo de mi infancia.
Hoy cuando el sol comenzó con sus espigas
a contar el relato más claro y más antiguo
como una cimitarra cayó la oblicua lluvia,
la lluvia que agradece mi corazón amargo.

Tú, mi bella, dormida aún en agosto,
mi reina, mi mujer, mi extensión, geografía,
beso de barro, cítara que cubren los carbones,
tú, vestidura de mi porfiado canto,
hoy otra vez renaces y con el agua negra
del cielo me confundes y me obligas:
debo reanudar mis huesos en tu reino,
debo aclarar aún mis deberes terrestres.

I

Today is that day, the day that carried
a desperate light that since has died.
Don't let the squatters know:
let's keep it all between us,
day, between your bell
and my secret.

Today is dead winter in the forgotten land
that comes to visit me, with a cross on the map
and a volcano in the snow, to return to me,
to return again the water
fallen on the roof of my childhood.
Today when the sun began with its shafts
to tell the story, so clear, so old,
the slanting rain fell like a sword,
the rain my hard heart welcomes.

You, my love, still asleep in August,
my queen, my woman, my vastness, my geography,
kiss of mud, the carbon-coated zither,
you, vestment of my persistent song,
today you are reborn again and with the sky's
black water confuse me and compel me:
I must renew my bones in your kingdom,
I must still uncloud my earthly duties.

II

Araucanía, rosa mojada, diviso
adentro de mí mismo o en las provincias del agua
tus raíces, las copas de los desenterrados,
con los alerces rotos, las araucarias muertas,
y tu nombre reluce en mis capítulos
como los peces pescados en el canasto amarillo!
Eres también patria plateada y hueles mal,
a rencor, a borrasca, a escalofrío.

Hoy que un día creció para ser ancho
como la tierra o más extenso aún,
cuando se abrió la luz mostrando el territorio
llegó tu lluvia y trajo en sus espadas
el retrato de ayer acribillado,
el amor de la tierra insoportable,
con aquellos caminos que me llevan
al Polo Sur, entre árboles quemados.

Araucanía, wet rose, I discover
inside myself, in the provinces of water
your roots, the goblets of the exhumed,
with the broken larches, the dead araucarias,
and your name shines in my chapters
like a catch of fish in the yellow creel!
You are also silver motherland and stink
in bitterness in storms in chills.

Today as a day grew wide
like the land and wider still,
when the light opened to illumine the land,
your rain came and brought in its swords
the portrait of bullet-riddled yesterday,
the love of the unbearable earth,
with those roads that carry me
to the South Pole, among burnt trees.

III

Invierna, Araucanía, Lonquimaya!
Leviathana, Archipiélaga, Oceana!

Pienso que el español de zapatos morados
montado en la invasión como en la náusea,
en su caballo como en una ola,
el descubridor, bajó de su Guatemala,
de los pasteles de maíz con olor a tumba,
de aquel calor de parto que inunda las Antillas,
para llegar aquí, de descalabro en derrota,
para perder la espada, la pared, la Santísima,
y luego perder los pies y las piernas
y el alma.
Ahora en este 65 que cumplo
mirando hacia atrás,
hacia arriba,
hacia abajo,
me puse a descubrir descubridores.
Pasa Colón con el primer colibrí
(pájaro de pulsera), relampaguito,
pasa don Pedro de Valdivia sin sombrero
y luego, de regreso, sin cabeza,
pasa Pizarro entre otros hombres tristes.
Y también don Alonso, el claro Ercilla.

III

Invierna, Araucanía, Lonquimaya!
Leviathana, Archipiélaga, Oceana!

I see that the purple-shoed Spaniard
climbed on the invasion as if on nausea,
climbed on his horse as if on a wave,
the discoverer stepped down from his Guatemala,
from the corncakes smelling of graves,
from the heat of birth flooding the Antilles,
to arrive here, from being wounded in defeat,
to lose his sword, his wall, his "precious virgin,"
and then to lose his feet, his legs,
and his soul.
Now that I am 65
looking back,
looking up,
looking down,
I settle in to discover the discoverers.
Columbus passes with the first hummingbird
(bird on the wrist), little lightning bolt,
don Pedro de Valdivia passes hatless
and later returns, headless,
Pizarro passes among other sad men.
And also don Alonso, the gallant Ercilla.

IV

Ercilla el ramificado, el polvoroso,
el diamantino, el pobre caballero,
por estas aguas anduvo, navegó estos caminos,
y aunque les pareció petimetre a los buitres
y éstos lo devolvieron, como carta sobrante,
a España pedregosa y polvorienta,
él solamente solo nos descubrió a nosotros:
sólo este abundantísimo palomo
se enmarañó en nosotros hasta ahora
y nos dejó en su testamento
un duradero amor ensangrentado.

IV

Ercilla, the multi-limbed, the dusty,
the diamond, the poor knight,
he walked these waters, navigated these roads,
and though he looked like a dandy to the vultures
and they sent him back, a discard,
to rocky, dusty Spain,
he alone discovered us:
only this prolific dove
tangled inside us till now,
who left us in his will
a lasting bloodstained love.

V

Bueno pues, llegaron otros:
eximios, medidores, chilenos meditativos
que hicieron casas húmedas en que yo me crié
y levantaron la bandera chilena
en aquel frío para que se helara,
en aquel viento para que viviera,
en plena lluvia para que llorara.
Se llenó el mundo de carabineros,
aparecieron las ferreterías,
los paraguas
fueron las nuevas aves regionales:
mi padre me regaló una capa
desde su poncho invicto de Castilla
y hasta llegaron libros
a la Frontera como se llamó
aquel capítulo que yo no escribí
sino que me escribieron.

Los araucanos se volvieron raíz!
Les fueron quitando hojas
hasta que sólo fueron esqueleto
de raza, o árbol ya destituido,
y no fue tanto el sufrimiento antiguo
puesto que ellos pelearon como vertiginosos,
como piedras, como sacos, como ángeles,
sino que ahora ellos, los honorarios,
sintieron que el terreno les faltaba,
la tierra se les iba de los pies:
ya había reinado en Arauco la sangre:
llegó el reino del robo:
y los ladrones éramos nosotros.

V

And then, others arrived:
VIPs, surveyors, contemplative Chileans
who built the damp houses in which I grew up
and who raised the Chilean flag
in cold that it might freeze,
in wind that it might live,
in hard rain that it might cry.
They filled the world with police,
the hardware stores appeared,
the umbrellas
were the new regional birds:
my father made me a cape
from his pure poncho of Castile
and even some books arrived
at the Frontier called
that chapter I'll never write
that someone wrote for me.

The Araucanians turned into roots.
They were stripped off leaf by leaf
until they were only a skeleton
of the race, a tree already leafless:
it wasn't so much the ancient suffering —
they were fighting like madmen,
like stones, like sacks, like angels;
it was that they, the brave ones,
felt themselves losing ground,
the earth giving under their feet:
the blood no longer reigned in Arauco:
the kingdom of theft had arrived
and we were the thieves.

VI

Perdón si cuando quiero
contar mi vida
es tierra lo que cuento.
Esta es la tierra.
Crece en tu sangre
y creces.
Si se apaga en tu sangre
tú te apagas.

VI

Pardon me, if when I want
to tell the story of my life
it's the land I talk about.
This is the land.
It grows in your blood
and you grow.
If it dies in your blood
you die out.

VII

Yumbel!
Yumbel, Yumbel!
De dónde
salió tu nombre al sol?
Por qué la luz
tintinea en tu nombre?
Por qué, por la mañana
tu nombre como un aro
sale sonando de las herrerías?

Yumbel!
Yumbel, Yumbel!
From where does your name
come out into the sunshine?
Why does the light
ring in your name?
Why, in the morning
does your name, like the rim of a wheel,
come sounding from the blacksmiths' shops?

VIII

Angol sucede seco
como un golpe de pájaro
en la selva,
como un canto
de hacha desnuda
que le pega a un roble.
Angol, Angol, Angol,
hacha profunda,
canto
de piedra pura
en la montaña,
clave de las herencias,
palabra como el vuelo
del halcón enlutado,
centrífugo, fugante
en las almenas
de la noche nevada!

VIII

Angol echoes dry
like the thump of a bird
in the woods,
like the song of a naked ax
sinking into an oak.
Angol, Angol, Angol,
ax that cuts deep,
song
of pure stone
in the mountain,
key of the legacies,
word like the flight
of the mourning falcon,
centrifugal, escaping
in the battlements
of the snowy night.

IX

Temuco, corazón de agua,
patrimonio
del digital: antaño
tu casa arbórea
fueron cuna y campana
de mi canto
y fortaleza
de mi soledad.

IX

Temuco, heart of water,
heritage
of foxglove: long ago
your house in the wood
was cradle and bell
of my song
and fortress
of my solitude.

X

Boroa clara,
manzana cristalina
y elemento
de la fecundidad, yo sigo
tus recostadas sílabas
irse en el río,
irse,
en el transcurso
de la plata sombría
que corre en la frescura.

X

Clear Boroa,
crystalline apple
and element
of fertility, I follow
your song that rests
in the running river,
in the passage
of shadows on silver
that flow in the cool.

XI

Arpa de Osorno bajo los volcanes!
Suenan las cuerdas oscuras
arrancadas al bosque.
Mírate en el espejo de madera!
Consúmete
en la más poderosa
fragancia del otoño
cuando las ramas dejan
caer hoja por hoja
un planeta amarillo
y sube sangre para que los volcanes
preparen fuego cada día.

XI

Harp of Osorno beneath the volcanoes!
Your dark strings sound
the uprooting of the woods.
Look at yourself in the mirror of wood!
Burn yourself
in the most powerful
fragrance of autumn
when the branches drop
a yellow planet
leaf by leaf
and blood rises so the volcanoes
will make fire every day.

Torre fría del mundo,
volcán, dedo de nieve
que me siguió por toda la existencia:
sobre la nave mía el mastelero
y aún oh primavera atolondrada,
viajero intermitente,
en el arañadero
de Buenos Aires, lejos
de donde me hice yo,
de donde me hice mí,
en Katiabar, en Sandokán, en Praga,
en Mollendo, en Toledo, en Guayaquil
con mi volcán a cuestas,
con mi nieve,
con fuego austral y noche calcinada,
con lenguas de volcán, con lava lenta
devorando la estrella.
Igneo deudor, compañero de nieve,
a donde fui conmigo
fui contigo,
torre de las secretas neverías,
fábrica de las llamas patriarcales.

XII

Cold tower of the world,
volcano, finger of snow
that followed me through all I did:
the topmast high above my ship
and yet O stunned spring,
intermittent traveler,
in the spider's nest
of Buenos Aires, far
from where I grew up,
where I became me,
in Katihar, in Sandakan, in Prague,
in Mollendo, in Toledo, in Guayaquil,
with my volcano on my back,
with my snow,
with southern fire and calcified night,
with volcanic tongues, with slow lava
devouring the star.
Igneous debtor, companion of snow,
where I went with me
I went with you,
tower of the secret icehouses,
factory of the patriarchal flames.

XIII

Crece el hombre con todo lo que crece
y se acrecienta Pedro con su río,
con el árbol que sube sin hablar
por eso mi palabra crece
y crece:
viene de aquel silencio con raíces,
de los días del trigo,
de aquellos gérmenes intransferibles,
del agua extensa,
del sol cerrado sin su consentimiento,
de los caballos sudando en la lluvia.

XIII

Men grow with all that grows
and Pedro rises with his river,
with the tree that climbs without words,
for this my word grows
and grows:
it comes from that silence with roots,
from the days of wheat,
from those untransferable germs,
from the vast water,
from the closed sun without its consent,
from the horses sweating in the rain.

XIV

Todos me reclamaban,
me decían «Idiota,
quédate aquí. Está tibia
la cama en el jardín
y a tu balcón se asoman
los jazmines, honor
de Europa, el vino
suave toro
sube hasta el Partenón, Racine dirige
los árboles rimados y Petrarca
sigue siendo de mármol y de oro».

No pude ir sin volver a parte alguna:
la tierra me prestaba, me perdía
y pronto, tarde ya, golpeaba el muro
o desde un pájaro me reclamaba.
Me sentí vagamente tricolor
y el penetrante signo del ají,
ciertas comidas, los tomates frescos,
las guitarras de octubre, las ciudades
inconclusas, las páginas del bosque
no leídas aún en sus totales:
aquella catarata
que en el salvaje Aysén cae partiendo
una roca en dos senos salpicados
por la blancura torrencial, la luna
en las tablas podridas de Loncoche,
el olor a mercado pobre, a cholga seca,
a iglesia, a alerce, allá en el archipiélago,
mi casa, mi Partido, en el fuego de cada día,

XIV

They were all calling me,
they said to me, "Stupid,
stay here. The bed in the garden
is warm
and at your balcony the jasmine
appears, the honor
of Europe, the wine
gentle bull
climbs as far as the Parthenon, Racine conducts
the rhyming trees and Petrarch
is still made of gold and marble."

I was unable to go anywhere without returning to it:
the earth lent me out, lost me
and soon, late by now, it would strike the wall
or call me from a bird.
I was distant kin to the tricolor,
and the penetrating sign of the chili,
certain foods, those fresh tomatoes,
the guitars of October, the unfinished
cities, the pages of the forest
still unread in their entirety:
that waterfall
in the wild Aysén plunges splitting
with its torrential whiteness a rock
into two speckled breasts, the moon
reflected on the rotten boards of Loncoche,
the smell of the poor marketplace, of dried clams,
of church, of larch tree, there in the archipelago,
my house, my Party, in the burning of each day,

y tú misma sureña, compañera de mi alma,
patrona de mis ojos, centinela,
todo lo que se llama lluvia y se llama patria,
lo que te ignora y te hiere y te acaricia a veces,
todo eso, un rumor cada semana más abierto,
cada noche más estrellado, cada vez más preciso,
me hizo volver y quedarme y no volver a partir:
que sepa todo el mundo que por lo menos en mí
la tierra me propone, me dispone y me embarga.

and yourself southerner, friend of my soul,
patroness of my eyes, sentinel,
all that is called rain and motherland,
all that ignores and wounds and caresses you,
all that, a murmur grown more open each week,
each night more starry, each time more precise,
it made me come back, and stay, and not go:
let the whole world know that at least in me
the earth proposes to me, uses me, and seizes me.

XV

Nosotros, los perecederos, tocamos los metales,
el viento, las orillas del océano, las piedras,
sabiendo que seguirán, inmóviles o ardientes,
y yo fui descubriendo, nombrando todas las cosas:
fue mi destino amar y despedirme.

XV

We, the mortals, touch the metals,
the wind, the ocean shores, the stones,
knowing they will go on, inert or burning,
and I was discovering, naming all these things:
it was my destiny to love and say goodbye.

XVI

Cada uno en el saco más oculto guardó
las alhajas perdidas del recuerdo,
intenso amor, noches secretas o besos permanentes,
el trozo de dicha pública o privada.
Algunos, retozones, coleccionaron caderas,
otros hombres amaron la madrugada escarbando
cordilleras o témpanos, locomotoras, números.
Para mí la dicha fue compartir cantando,
alabando, imprecando, llorando con mil ojos.
Pido perdón por mi mal comportamiento:
no tuvo utilidad mi gestión en la tierra.

XVI

Each in the most hidden sack kept
the lost jewels of memory,
intense love, secret nights and permanent kisses,
the fragment of public or private happiness.
A few, the wolves, collected thighs,
other men loved the dawn scratching
mountain ranges or ice floes, locomotives, numbers.
For me happiness was to share singing,
praising, cursing, crying with a thousand eyes.
I ask forgiveness for my bad ways:
my life had no use on earth.

XVII

Fue temblorosa la noche de setiembre.
Yo traía en mi ropa
la tristeza del tren que me traía
cruzando una por una las provincias:
yo era ese ser remoto
turbado por el humo del carbón
de la locomotora.
Yo no era.
Tuve que ver entonces con la vida.
Mi poesía me incomunicaba
y me agregaba a todos.
Aquella noche a mí
me tocó declarar la Primavera.
A mí, pobre sombrío,
me hicieron desatar la vestimenta
de la noche desnuda.
Temblé leyendo ante dos mil orejas desiguales
mi canto.
La noche ardió
con todo el fuego oscuro
que se multiplicaba en la ciudad,
en la urgencia imperiosa del contacto.

Murió la soledad aquella vez?
O nací entonces, de mi soledad?

XVII

The September night was trembling.
I carried in my clothes
the sadness of the train that carried me
across the provinces one by one:
I was that distant being
sickened by the carbon fumes
of the locomotive.
I didn't exist, yet.
I had something to discover.
My poetry isolated me
and joined me to everyone.
That night I would
have declared Spring.
A sad beggar,
I was made to untie the vestment
of the naked night.
I trembled reading my song before two thousand
uneven ears.
The night burned
with all the dark fire
that multiplied in the city,
in the urgent need of contact.

Did the loneliness die that night?
Or was I born then, of my solitude?

XVIII

Los días no se descartan ni se suman, son abejas
que ardieron de dulzura o enfurecieron
el aguijón: el certamen continúa,
van y vienen los viajes desde la miel al dolor.
No, no se deshila la red de los años: no hay red.
No caen gota a gota desde un río: no hay río.
El sueño no divide la vida en dos mitades,
ni la acción, ni el silencio, ni la virtud:
fue como una piedra la vida, un solo movimiento,
una sola fogata que reverberó en el follaje,
una flecha, una sola, lenta o activa, un metal
que ascendió y descendió quemándose en tus huesos.

XVIII

The days aren't discarded or collected, they are bees
that burned with sweetness or maddened
the sting: the struggle continues,
the journeys go and come between honey and pain.
No, the net of the years doesn't unweave: there is no net.
They don't fall drop by drop from a river: there is no river.
Sleep doesn't divide life into halves,
or action, or silence, or honor:
life is like a stone, a single motion,
a lonesome bonfire reflected on the leaves,
an arrow, only one, slow or swift, a metal
that climbs or descends burning in your bones.

XIX

Mi abuelo don José Angel Reyes vivió
ciento dos años entre Parral y la muerte.
Era un gran caballero campesino
con poca tierra y demasiados hijos.
De cien años de edad lo estoy viendo: nevado
era este viejo, azul era su antigua barba
y aún entraba en los trenes para verme crecer,
en carro de tercera, de Cauquenes al Sur.
Llegaba el sempiterno don José Angel, el viejo,
a tomar una copa, la última, conmigo:
su mano de cien años levantaba
el vino que temblaba como una mariposa.

XIX

Don José Angel Reyes, my grandfather, lived
a hundred and two years between Parral and death.
He was a gentleman peasant
with little land and too many children.
I see him at a hundred years:
this old man was snowcapped, his old beard blue
and still he came by train to watch me grow,
in a third-class car, from Cauquenes to the South.
The eternal don José Angel, the old man arrived
to have a drink, his last one, with me:
in his hundred-year-old hand
the raised wine fluttered like a butterfly.

XX

Otras cosas he visto, tal vez nada, países
purpúreos, estuarios que traían del útero
de la tierra, el olor seminal del origen,
países ferruginosos con cuevas de diamantes
(ciudad Bolívar, allá en el Orinoco)
y en otro reino estuve, de color amaranto
en que todos y todas eran reyes y reinas
de color amaranto.

XX

I have seen other things, perhaps nothing, purple
countries, estuaries that carried from the womb
of the land, the seminal odor of origin,
iron rust countries with caves of diamonds
(the city of Bolívar, there in the Orinoco)
and I was in another kingdom, of the color of amaranth
where men and women all were kings and queens
the color of amaranth.

XXI

Yo viví en la baraja de patrias no nacidas,
en colonias que aún no sabían nacer,
con banderas inéditas que se ensangrentarían.
Yo viví en el fogón de pueblos malheridos
comiendo el pan extraño con mi padecimiento.

XXI

I lived in the shuffle of unborn motherlands,
in colonies that still didn't know how to be born,
with undrawn flags that would soon be bloodied.
I lived by the campfire of badly wounded towns
and devoured my own anguish like strange bread.

XXII

Alguna vez, cerca de Antofagasta,
entre las malgastadas vidas del hombre
y el círculo arenoso
de la pampa,
sin ver ni oír me detuve en la nada:
el aire es vertical en el desierto:
no hay animales (ni siquiera moscas)
sólo la tierra, como la luna, sin caminos,
sólo la plenitud inferior del planeta,
los kilómetros densos de noche y material.
Yo allí solo, buscando la razón de la tierra
sin hombres y sin alas, poderosa,
sola en su magnitud, como si hubiera
destruido una por una las vidas
para establecer su silencio.

XXII

One time, near Antofagasta,
between the squandered lives of men
and the sandy circle
of the pampas,
not hearing or seeing anything, I stopped in nothingness:
the air is vertical in the desert:
there are no animals (not even flies)
only the earth, like the moon, without roads,
only the lower vastness of the planet,
the dense kilometers of night and matter.
There alone I sought the purpose of a land
without men or wings, powerful,
single in its reach, as if it had
destroyed one by one those lives
to impose its silence.

XXIII

Arenas de Isla Negra, cinturón,
estrella demolida, cinta de la certeza:
el peligro del mar azota con su rosa
la piedra desplegada de la costa.
Abrupta estirpe, litoral combate!
Hasta Quebrada Verde, por el frío,
como un diamante se detuvo el día
poderoso, como un avión azul.

El sol nuevo amontona sus espadas
desde abajo y enciende el horizonte
rompiendo ola por ola su dominio.
Arrugas del conflicto! Quebrada
de Mirasol, por donde
corrió el carro glacial del ventisquero
dejando esta cortante cicatriz:
el mar abajo muere y agoniza
y nace y muere y muere
y nace y muere y nace.

XXIII

Sands of Isla Negra, belt,
smashed star, ribbon of certainty:
with its rose the peril of the sea
beats the unfolded stone of the coast.
Craggy bloodline, coastal combat!
As far as Quebrada Verde, from the cold,
the day pauses, a powerful diamond,
a blue plane.

From below the new sun collects its swords
and wave by wave lights up the horizon
breaking over its dominion.
Wrinkles of conflict! Quebrada
de Mirasol, through which the icy
cart of the glacier passes
leaving this biting scar:
the sea below dies and agonizes
is born and dies and dies
is born and dies and is born.

XXIV

La Ballenera de Quintay, vacía
con sus bodegas, sus escombros muertos,
la sangre aún sobre las rocas, los
huesos de los monárquicos cetáceos,
hierro roído, viento y mar, el graznido
del albatros que espera.

Se fueron las ballenas: a otro mar?
Huyeron de la costa encarnizada?
O sumergidas en el suave lodo
de la profundidad piden castigo
para los oceánicos chilenos?

Y nadie defendió a las gigantescas!

Hoy, en el mes de Julio
resbalo aún en el aceite helado:
se me van los zapatos hacia el Polo
como si las presencias invisibles
me empujaran al mar,
y una melancolía grave como el invierno
va llevando mis pies
por la deshabitada Ballenera.

XXIV

The whaling town of Quintay, empty
with its warehouses, its dead debris,
the blood still upon the rocks,
the bones of the kingly cetaceans,
eaten iron, wind and sea, the screech
of the waiting albatross.

The whales left for another sea?
Did they escape the bloody coast?
Or, submerged in the fine sludge
of the depths, do they call for punishment
of the seafaring Chileans?

And no one defended the giants!

Today, in the month of July,
I still slip on the frozen oil:
my shoes turn toward the Pole
as if the invisible spirits
were pushing me out to sea,
and a heavy melancholy like winter
is making off with my feet
through the deserted port.

XXV

Se va el hoy. Fue una cápsula
de fría luz que volvió a su recinto,
a su madre sombría, a renacer.
Lo dejo ahora envuelto en su linaje.
Es verdad, día, que participé en la luz?
Tiempo, soy parte de tu catarata?
Arenas mías, soledades!

Si es verdad que nos vamos,
nos fuimos consumiendo
a plena sal marina
y a golpes de relámpago.
Mi razón ha vivido a la intemperie,
entregué al mar ni corazón calcáreo.

XXV

This day departs. It was a seed
of cold light that returned to its pod,
to its dark mother, to be born again.
I leave it now wrapped in its lineage.
Is it true, day, that I lived in the light?
Time, am I part of your cataract?
My sands, solitudes!

If it's true we go,
we went, were consumed
in the middle of the salty sea
by flashes of lightning.
My reason survived bitter weather,
I surrendered to the sea my calcareous heart.

XXVI

Si hay una piedra devorada
en ella tengo parte:
estuve yo en la ráfaga,
en la ola,
en el incendio terrestre.

Respeta esa piedra perdida.

Si hallas en un camino
a un niño
robando manzanas
y a un viejo sordo
con un acordeón,
recuerda que yo soy
el niño, las manzanas y el anciano.
No me hagas daño persiguiendo al niño,
no le pegues al viejo vagabundo,
no eches al río las manzanas.

XXVI

If ever a stone was devoured
I am a part of it:
I was in the squall,
in the wave,
in the earthly fire.

Honor the stone that was lost.

If on a road you find
a boy
stealing apples
and a deaf old man
with an accordion,
remember that I am
the boy, the apples, and that old man.
Do not harm me by chasing the boy,
do not strike the old bum,
do not throw apples in the river.

XXVII

Hasta aquí estoy.
Estamos.
Los lineales, los encarnizados,
los sombrereros que pasaron la vida
midiendo mi cabeza y tu cabeza,
los cinturistas
que se pegaban a cada cintura,
a cada teta del mundo.
Aquí vamos a seguir codo a codo
con los anacoretas,
con el joven con su tierna indigestión de guerrillas,
con los tradicionales que se ofuscaban
porque nadie quería comer mierda.
Pero además,
honor del día fresco,
la juventud del rocío,
la mañana del mundo,
lo que crece a pesar
del tiempo amargo:
el orden puro
que necesitamos.

XXVII

Still, I am here.
We all are.
The good citizens, the bloodthirsty,
the hatmakers who passed through life
measuring my head and your head,
the beltmakers
who stuck to each waist,
to each breast of the world.
We're going to line up elbow to elbow
with the anchorites,
the young with the indigestion of guerrillas,
with the traditionalists who were bewildered
because nobody wanted to eat shit.
But moreover,
integrity of the new day,
youth of the dew,
morning of the world,
whatever else grows despite
the bitter weather:
we need pure order.

XXVIII

Hasta luego, invitado.
Buenos días.
Sucedió mi poema
para ti, para nadie,
para todos.

Voy a rogarte: déjame intranquilo.
Vivo con el océano intratable
y me cuesta mucho el silencio.

Me muero con cada ola cada día.
Me muero con cada día en cada ola.
Pero el día no muere
nunca.
No muere.
Y la ola?
No muere.

Gracias.

XXVIII

So long, visitor.
Good day.
My poem happened
for you, for nobody,
for everyone.

I beg you: leave me restless.
I live with the impossible ocean
and silence bleeds me dry.

I die with each wave each day.
I die with each day in each wave.
But the day does not die—
not ever.
It does not die.
And the wave?
It does not die.

Gracias.

ABOUT THE AUTHOR

Pablo Neruda was born Neftalí Ricardo Reyes Basoalto in Parral, Chile, in 1904. He served as consul in Burma (now Myanmar) and held diplomatic posts in various East Asian and European countries. In 1945, a few years after he joined the Communist Party, Neruda was elected to the Chilean Senate. Shortly thereafter, when Chile's political climate took a sudden turn to the right, Neruda fled to Mexico and lived as an exile for several years. He later established a permanent home at Isla Negra. In 1970 he was appointed Chile's ambassador to France, and in 1971 he was awarded the Nobel Prize in Literature. Pablo Neruda died in 1973.

About the Translator

William O'Daly, who is a poet, teacher, instructional designer, and editor, spent seventeen years translating the late and posthumous poetry of Pablo Neruda. He has published six books of Neruda translations with Copper Canyon Press as well as a chapbook of his own poems, *The Whale in the Web*. He recently completed a historical novel set in China, co-authored with the Chinese writer Hanping Chin. Raised in Los Angeles, California, O'Daly currently resides with his wife and daughter in the foothills of the northern Sierra Nevada.

OTHER BOOKS BY PABLO NERUDA
FROM COPPER CANYON PRESS

The Separate Rose
translated by William O'Daly

Winter Garden
translated by William O'Daly

The Sea and the Bells
translated by William O'Daly

Stones of the Sky
translated by James Nolan

The Yellow Heart
translated by William O'Daly

The Book of Questions
translated by William O'Daly

*Copper Canyon Press wishes to acknowledge the support of
Lannan Foundation in funding the publication and distribution
of exceptional literary works.*

LANNAN LITERARY SELECTIONS 2005

June Jordan, *Directed by Desire*
W.S. Merwin, *Migration*
W.S. Merwin, *Present Company*
Pablo Neruda, *The Separate Rose*
Pablo Neruda, *Still Another Day*
Alberto Ríos, *The Theater of Night*

LANNAN LITERARY SELECTIONS 2000–2004

John Balaban, *Spring Essence: The Poetry of Hồ Xuân Hương*
Marvin Bell, *Rampant*
Hayden Carruth, *Doctor Jazz*
Cyrus Cassells, *More Than Peace and Cypresses*
Norman Dubie, *The Mercy Seat: Collected & New Poems,
1967–2001*
Sascha Feinstein, *Misterioso*
James Galvin, *X: Poems*
Jim Harrison, *The Shape of the Journey: New and Collected Poems*
Maxine Kumin, *Always Beginning: Essays on a Life in Poetry*
Ben Lerner, *The Lichtenberg Figures*

Antonio Machado, *Border of a Dream: Selected Poems*,
translated by Willis Barnstone

W.S. Merwin, *The First Four Books of Poems*

Cesare Pavese, *Disaffections: Complete Poems 1930–1950*,
translated by Geoffrey Brock

Antonio Porchia, *Voices*, translated by W.S. Merwin

Kenneth Rexroth, *The Complete Poems*,
edited by Sam Hamill and Bradford Morrow

Alberto Ríos, *The Smallest Muscle in the Human Body*

Theodore Roethke, *On Poetry & Craft*

Ann Stanford, *Holding Our Own: The Selected Poems*,
edited by Maxine Scates and David Trinidad

Ruth Stone, *In the Next Galaxy*

Joseph Stroud, *Country of Light*

Rabindranath Tagore, *The Lover of God*,
translated by Tony K. Stewart and Chase Twichell

Reversible Monuments: Contemporary Mexican Poetry,
edited by Mónica de la Torre and Michael Wiegers

César Vallejo, *The Black Heralds*, translated by Rebecca Seiferle

Eleanor Rand Wilner, *The Girl with Bees in Her Hair*

C.D. Wright, *Steal Away: Selected and New Poems*

For more on the Lannan Literary Selections, visit:
www.coppercanyonpress.org

The Chinese character for poetry is made up of two parts: "word" and "temple." It also serves as pressmark for Copper Canyon Press.

Founded in 1972, Copper Canyon Press remains dedicated to publishing poetry exclusively, from Nobel laureates to new and emerging authors. The Press thrives with the generous patronage of readers, writers, booksellers, librarians, teachers, students, and funders—everyone who shares the conviction that poetry invigorates the language and sharpens our appreciation of the world.

MAJOR FUNDING HAS BEEN PROVIDED BY:

The Paul G. Allen Family Foundation
Lannan Foundation
National Endowment for the Arts
Washington State Arts Commission

FOR INFORMATION AND CATALOGS:
Copper Canyon Press
Post Office Box 271
Port Townsend, Washington 98368
360-385-4925
www.coppercanyonpress.org

Printed in the USA
CPSIA information can be obtained
at www.ICGtesting.com
JSHW012047140824
68134JS00034B/3307